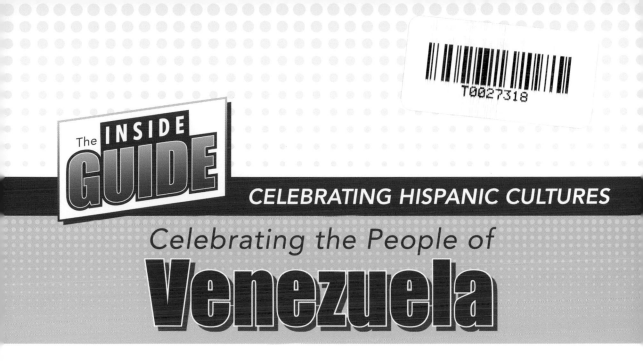

The **INSIDE GUIDE**

CELEBRATING HISPANIC CULTURES

Celebrating the People of

Venezuela

By Rosie Banks

Cavendish Square

New York

Published in 2023 by Cavendish Square Publishing, LLC
29 E. 21st Street New York, NY 10010

Website: cavendishsq.com

Library of Congress Cataloging-in-Publication Data

Names: Banks, Rosie, 1978- author.
Title: Celebrating the people of Venezuela / Rosie Banks.
Description: New York : Cavendish Square Publishing, [2023] | Series: The inside guide: celebrating Hispanic cultures | Includes index.
Identifiers: LCCN 2021041343 (print) | LCCN 2021041344 (ebook) | ISBN 9781502664709 (library binding) | ISBN 9781502664686 (paperback) | ISBN 9781502664693 (set) | ISBN 9781502664716 (ebook)
Subjects: LCSH: Venezuela–Juvenile literature. | Venezuela–Civilization–Juvenile literature.
Classification: LCC F2308.5 .B36 2023 (print) | LCC F2308.5 (ebook) | DDC 987–dc23
LC record available at https://lccn.loc.gov/2021041343
LC ebook record available at https://lccn.loc.gov/2021041344

Editor: Therese Shea
Copyeditor: Jill Keppeler
Designer: Deanna Paternostro

The photographs in this book are used by permission and through the courtesy of: Cover AJR_photo/Shutterstock.com; p. 4 testing/Shutterstock.com; p. 5 Vadim Petrakov/Shutterstock.com; p. 7 Douglas Olivares/Shutterstock.com; p. 8 (inset) JohannaWallace/Shutterstock.com; pp. 8–9 Elena Lebedeva-Hooft/Shutterstock.com; p. 10 Moises Abraham/Shutterstock.com; p. 13 Erik Gonzalez/Shutterstock.com; p. 14 (top, bottom) nehophoto/Shutterstock.com; pp. 16, 17 Paolo Costa/Shutterstock.com; p. 18 casa.da.photo/Shutterstock.com; p. 19 neftali/Shutterstock.com; p. 20 (main and inset) Giongi63/Shutterstock.com; p. 21 parksfotografia/Shutterstock.com; pp. 22, 29 (right) Roberto Galan/Shutterstock.com; p. 24 Keeton Gale/Shutterstock.com; p. 26 Janusz Pienkowski/Shutterstock.com; p. 27 Angel Corrales/Shutterstock.com; p. 28 (flag) patrice6000/Shutterstock.com; p. 28 (map) Andrei Minsk/Shutterstock.com; p. 29 (left) slowmotiongli/Shutterstock.com; p. 29 (center) Alejandro Solo/Shutterstock.com.

Some of the images in this book illustrate individuals who are models. The depictions do not imply actual situations or events.

CPSIA compliance information: Batch #CSCSQ23: For further information contact Cavendish Square Publishing LLC, New York, New York, at 1-877-980-4450.

Printed in the United States of America

Find us on

CONTENTS

Venezuela has mountains, waterfalls (such as the one on the opposite page), and Lake Maracaibo—one of the largest lakes in South America. It has urban areas too. This is the capital city of Caracas.

HISTORY AND DIVERSITY

The Bolivarian **Republic** of Venezuela—better known as simply Venezuela—is filled with varied landscapes and natural resources that add to its considerable beauty. The culture of this South American country is the result of different traditions coming together. After colonization began in the 1500s, Spanish, African, and **indigenous** cultures began to blend. Most Venezuelans can trace their family back to a combination of these **heritages**.

More than 29 million people live and work in Venezuela today. Though the country's past—as well as its present—is marked with periods of conflict and struggle, its people still maintain

Fast Fact

Venezuela is sometimes called a Hispanic country because most of its people speak Spanish. However, many Venezuelans speak indigenous languages too.

a culture of rich traditions. A look back at Venezuela's history reveals the roots of some of its customs.

Tierra de Gracia

On Christopher Columbus's third voyage to the Americas, he landed in Venezuela while exploring the Gulf of Paria in 1498. He was amazed by the area's beauty. He called it Tierra de Gracia, which means "Land of Grace."

Venezuela is located on the northern coast of South America. It has about 1,740 miles (2,800 kilometers) of coastline that touch the Caribbean Sea and the Atlantic Ocean. On the western side of the country, the Andes Mountains stretch toward the sea. Hills and valleys cover most of the southeast, with large *tepuis*—mountains with a flat top—bordering Brazil.

Venezuela features great biodiversity, which means the country is home to many plant and animal species. More than 350 species of mammals live in Venezuela, including jaguars, sloths, pumas, and howler monkeys. Venezuela is also home to the anaconda, the largest snake in the world.

Native Peoples

Long ago, Venezuela was home to many indigenous peoples, who built their communities in tropical jungles and along the coastline. The different landscapes of the country aided each group in developing its own **unique** culture.

Fast Fact

The capybara, a mammal found in Venezuela, is the largest rodent species on Earth.

One group, the Chibchas, lived in the Andes Mountains as farmers. They grew vegetables such as maize (corn) and potatoes. Along the rivers, the Warao lived as hunters and gatherers. The Añu built houses on

tepui

Angel Falls (Parecupá Merú), the highest waterfall in the world, is in the southeastern Guiana Highlands of Venezuela. It's 3,212 feet (979 meters) tall.

Fast Fact

European explorers named the country "Venezuela," which is Spanish for "little Venice," after finding indigenous people living in houses raised over lakes. (Venice is a city in Italy built on small islands.)

Shown here are members of an indigenous group called the Piaroa performing a traditional dance.

wooden poles above the waters of their coastal homes. Living near the water provided a steady source of food such as fish and other wildlife.

Many indigenous peoples still live in Venezuela today and make up a small percentage of the population. Most make their home in the Amazon rain forest, the Andes, and other distant parts of the country.

Some Warao still live near the Orinoco River in Venezuela. Shown here are traditional Warao homes.

SLAVERY IN VENEZUELA

In the late 1500s, Spanish explorers founded new settlements in Venezuela. They were hoping to become wealthy through trade and finding valuable items such as gold. They fought wars with the indigenous groups of the region. Native people often lost these battles, and the Europeans enslaved them. The Spanish conquest resulted in the **decimation** of the indigenous Venezuelans. Many died from European-carried diseases; others died of starvation and the harsh conditions of slavery. The first enslaved Africans were brought to Venezuela in 1528. The Spanish forced them to work on large farms called plantations. Slavery wasn't abolished, or outlawed, until 1854.

The majority of Venezuelans identify as Catholic. Churches like this one are found throughout the country.

CULTURAL TRADITIONS

As more colonists arrived in Venezuela, the cultures of indigenous groups mixed with Spanish, European, and African traditions. This resulted in new religious beliefs. Today, more than 90 percent of Venezuelans follow the Roman Catholic religion that the Spanish brought with them. This greatly influences the culture of the nation. People also practice Judaism, Islam, and indigenous religions.

Many Venezuelans also worship María Lionza. According to one tale, Lionza—the daughter of an indigenous leader and a European colonizer—lived on Sorte Mountain in central Venezuela in the 1400s. One day, as she was looking into a river, an anaconda ate her. From within the snake, she asked the mountain for help, and María Lionza and Sorte became one. Another tale says she wrestled the anaconda until it exploded. Either way, many people see her as a goddess. Her followers call for spirits to help them heal and see the future.

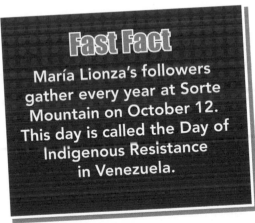

Fast Fact

María Lionza's followers gather every year at Sorte Mountain on October 12. This day is called the Day of Indigenous Resistance in Venezuela.

Holidays and Festivals

As Venezuela is mostly a Roman Catholic country, many of its holidays and festivals are connected to Catholic holy days. The most popular is Carnival, which is celebrated in the days before Ash Wednesday, the first day of **Lent**. A large parade marks the beginning of the celebration. People dress in impressive costumes, dance to favorite rhythms, and sing traditional songs.

Fast Fact

Venezuelan Independence Day is July 5. On this day in 1811, a congress of Venezuelan provinces declared freedom from Spain.

Christmas is a big celebration in Venezuela, with families decorating and singing in the evenings. Venezuelans celebrate Christmas from mid-December until January 6. Traditionally, it's believed that the Three Kings, who were said to have visited the baby Jesus Christ, bring gifts for children.

Other important festivals are held for patron saint days. Patron saints are religious figures believed to offer protection and guidance. Each Venezuelan village has its own patron saint and its special way of honoring that saint.

Popular Foods

Traditionally, Venezuelans are known to offer plentiful food to guests. Beans, rice, fruits, and vegetables are common in Venezuelan dishes, but recipes and ingredients vary across the country.

Arepas are fried or baked corn pancakes. They may have different fillings, including eggs and tomatoes or shrimp and cheese. Venezuelans snack on them, and small ones may be served as side

Visitors to Venezuela during Carnival will notice that the nation comes alive with bright colors and lively music during this time of celebration before the more serious days of Lent begin.

13

hallaca

cachapa

Cachapas are thick, sweet corn pancakes served with *queso guayanesa*, a cheese somewhat like mozzarella.

THE NATIONAL DISH

The national dish of Venezuela, *pabellón criollo*, is made with rice, black beans, and beef. The name means "**Creole** flag." The dish is placed on the plate so that the beef, black beans, and white rice resemble the three stripes of a flag. Pabellón criollo is considered a symbol of the indigenous, African, and European backgrounds of the Venezuelan population. It may also contain cheese, tomatoes, plantains, avocado, peppers, or fried eggs. Some Venezuelans put a bit of sugar on the beans too. It's generally an affordable and filling meal. Other Hispanic countries have similar dishes with slight variations.

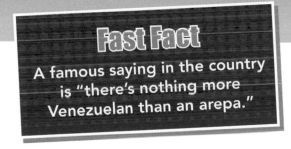

Fast Fact

A famous saying in the country is "there's nothing more Venezuelan than an arepa."

dishes. *Hallaca* is a dish of meat mixed with green peppers, garlic, onions, tomatoes, raisins, olives, herbs, and spices. Corn dough is wrapped around the mixture, and then it's steamed in banana leaves. It's typically served at Christmas.

Tequeños, a dish named for the city of Los Teques, are pastries filled with cheese or chocolate. During the Carnival season, there are even more complex dishes. Paella and *talkarí de chivo*, a kind of stew, are common.

The *Esfera Caracas* (Caracas Sphere) is a kinetic sculpture made from aluminum rods. They form an orange ball that looks like it's suspended in the air. It was created by the Venezuelan artist Jesús Soto.

THE ARTS

Hundreds of years ago, the indigenous peoples of Venezuela were the area's first artists. They created needed tools and items such as pottery, instruments, blankets, and baskets. Natural materials, such as coconut husks, palm fibers, and wool, were used to produce colorful folk art. Many of today's indigenous Venezuelans create the same types of art as their **ancestors**.

Religious traditions inspired much sculpture and painting in the 1800s, though this has changed in recent years. Many different styles influence modern Venezuelan artists, who often blend **abstract** elements into their work. Another style that has become popular is kinetic art, in which artists create pieces that move—or look like they move. It's common to see modern works of

Abra Solar kinetic sculpture in Caracas

Fast Fact

Venezuelans' interest in abstract and modern art is also seen in Caracas's architecture, or the design of its buildings.

art featuring bold colors and shapes in Venezuela.

Literature

Before Venezuela gained its independence from Spain, much of the literature of the country was about the government. This included the writings of Simón Bolívar (1783–1830), the head of the independence movement. After the country won its independence in the early 1800s, other genres, or styles, became popular.

The most popular genre in Venezuela is historical fiction. Many writers have

Simón Bolívar inspired people to follow him into battle against Spain. Six Latin American nations credit him with winning their freedom.

written about the Venezuelan War of Independence and the conquistadors—the Spanish soldiers who conquered parts of the Americas. Venezuela's most famous novel is *Doña Bárbara* by Rómulo Gallegos (1884–1969). It's about a cruel woman who lives on the plains of Venezuela.

Rómulo Gallegos

Arturo Uslar Pietri (1906–2001) was a Venezuelan novelist, journalist, and politician. He was one of the first Latin American writers to use magical realism, a style that adds unreal, or imaginary, features to everyday occurrences.

Music

The national music of Venezuela is joropo, which comes from a Spanish word meaning "party." Joropo is a style of folk music that combines elements of European, South American, and African music. It's part of a large group of styles called *música llanera* (music of the plains). It's traditionally played with a harp and maracas, though different regions of

Venezuelans celebrate the beginning of Semana Santa (Holy Week) before Easter with music in Caracas.

DANCE IN VENEZUELA

Indigenous peoples have historically used dance to celebrate festivals and feasts. These dances combined with those of early colonists to create the dances performed by Venezuelans today. Most modern Venezuelan festivals have some form of traditional music and dance featured in their celebrations. Ballet in Venezuela involves traditional dance as well as more modern styles. Ballet International de Caracas performed the joropo dance across Latin America and the United States in the 1970s, while many companies now perform classical forms of ballet. Today, the most popular kinds of dance are salsa and *cumbia*, which has a rhythm slower than salsa.

the country have other traditions. Joropo may be performed with poetry and dancing. Other folk music styles include *gaita*, which is played at festivals and Christmastime.

The cuatro, a four-string guitar, is the national instrument of Venezuela. The country is also home to many different styles of harps, which are traditionally used in folk music. Venezuelan music today combines Spanish, African, and indigenous influences. The most popular styles are salsa, merengue, and reggaeton.

cuatros

These young people display traditional Venezuelan clothing, including the *liqui-liqui* on the boy at left.

A CHANGING COUNTRY

If you traveled to Venezuela today, you'd see people who look much like you and your neighbors. Most Venezuelans wear Western-style clothing to keep them cool in their warm climate. Traditional Venezuelan clothing is usually worn only for special occasions.

The traditional outfit for men is called the *liqui-liqui,* which is a shirt and pants made of white cotton with gold buttons. It can also be fastened with leather or a sash. This outfit is similar to what the llanero, or traditional Venezuelan herdsmen, used to wear. Traditional clothing for women is ruffled blouses with long skirts. These skirts can come in any number of colors. For festivals, clothing can vary from traditional dress to elaborate and colorful costumes.

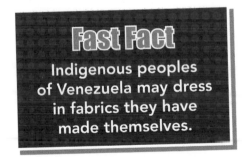

Fast Fact

Indigenous peoples of Venezuela may dress in fabrics they have made themselves.

Games and More

If you traveled to Venezuela today, you might also catch a ball game! Baseball is the official sport of Venezuela. As of 2021, eight teams play in Venezuela's professional baseball league. Many Venezuelan players

Miguel Cabrera is a Venezuelan first baseman for the Detroit Tigers of Major League Baseball (MLB). He's been an All-Star many times and has won the World Series too.

have gone on to play for American teams, including the New York Yankees, the Chicago Cubs, and the Cincinnati Reds. Other popular sports include soccer (called *fútbol*), basketball, and boxing.

Horse racing is a popular pastime, and Caracas has one of the finest racetracks in Latin America. Bullfighting is another favorite activity, and many Venezuelan cities have their own *plaza de toros* (bullring). In Caracas, about a dozen bullfights are held each year, usually around the festival of Carnival.

Recent Struggles

As much as Venezuela seems like other Hispanic countries in many ways, it faces more challenges than most. It was once the wealthiest country in South America. Now, it's the poorest. Its economy collapsed as oil prices dipped worldwide. Many Venezuelans lack food, medicine, and clean water.

Some have blamed the leadership of President Nicolás Maduro, accusing him of acting like a **dictator**. Others blame his **predecessor**, Hugo Chávez, for the policies he had put in place. Conditions in the nation became worse during the COVID-19 **pandemic.**

VENEZUELAN HEROES

Even in hardship, Venezuelans honor their historical heroes. Guaicaipuro (*shown below*) was an indigenous hero who lived in Los Teques and fought the Spanish for almost 10 years in the 1500s. Simón Bolívar, known as El Libertador (The Liberator), led the fight against Spanish rule in the early 1800s. His success led to Venezuelan independence in 1811. His birth is celebrated July 24 each year. After independence, many leaders worked hard to defend Venezuelan freedoms. Rómulo Betancourt, a revolutionary who opposed unfair laws in Venezuela, became president in 1945 and worked to improve the country. He's sometimes called the Father of Venezuelan **Democracy**.

More than 4.5 million Venezuelans have left the country since 2015. Most have gone to neighboring countries. The number of Venezuelan-born people in the United States has been growing, numbering more than 394,000 as of 2018.

In Venezuela, many streets and even a state are named for Simón Bolívar. Venezuela's currency, or kind of money, is called the bolívar soberano. Shown here is the National Pantheon of Venezuela (Panteón Nacional de Venezuela), which houses the remains of Bolívar.

Venezuelan culture will survive through its people's traditions, no matter where they live. Exploring rich cultures like this is one way to gain an appreciation for a unique heritage and the people who call it their own.

Kind of Government
federal presidential republic

Population
29,069,153 (estimate, 2021)

Total Area
352,144 square miles (912,050 sq km)

Capital City
Caracas

Official Country Name
Bolivarian Republic of Venezuela (República Bolivariana de Venezuela)

Kind of Money
bolívar soberano

Number of States
23

Flag

Location

THINK ABOUT IT!

1. Do you think the mixed heritage of most Venezuelans affects their lives? If so, how?

2. What impact might the economic situation in Venezuela have on parts of its culture?

3. What challenges might the country's economic problems create for indigenous people in particular?

4. Why do you think many Venezuelans choose to remain in their country, although conditions are difficult for them?

GLOSSARY

abstract: Describing art that doesn't represent reality but uses shapes, forms, colors, and textures to achieve its effect.

ancestor: A family member who lived long ago.

Creole: Referring to types of cooking and seasoned food common to Creole peoples, or those of European or African descent born in the West Indies or French or Spanish America.

decimation: The act of destroying something nearly completely.

democracy: A form of government in which all citizens can participate.

dictator: A person who rules a country with total power, often in a cruel way.

heritage: The traditions and beliefs that are part of the history of a group or nation.

indigenous: Having to do with the first peoples of an area.

Lent: The 40 days from Ash Wednesday to Easter observed by the Roman Catholic Church and some other churches as a period of prayer and fasting.

pandemic: An outbreak of a disease that occurs over a wide area.

predecessor: A person who has occupied a position before someone else.

republic: A form of government in which the people elect representatives who run the government.

unique: Being the only one of its kind.

FIND OUT MORE

Books

Anderson, Corey. *Hola, Venezuela*. Ann Arbor, MI: Cherry Lake Publishing, 2020.

Birdoff, Ariel Factor. *Venezuela*. Minneapolis, MN: Bearport Publishing Company, Inc., 2019.

Cruz, Bárbara. *Simón Bolívar: Fighting for Latin American Liberation*. New York, NY: Enslow Publishing, 2018.

Websites

Venezuela
www.cia.gov/the-world-factbook/countries/venezuela/
This CIA website gives a detailed account of the country.

Venezuela Facts for Kids
www.sciencekids.co.nz/sciencefacts/countries/venezuela.html
Read about Venezuela's population, history, land features, wildlife, and much more.

Venezuela Profile
www.bbc.com/news/world-latin-america-19652436
Check this timeline for recent events that may change Venezuela's future.

Publisher's note to educators and parents: Our editors have carefully reviewed these websites to ensure that they are suitable for students. Many websites change frequently, however, and we cannot guarantee that a site's future contents will continue to meet our high standards of quality and educational value. Be advised that students should be closely supervised whenever they access the internet.

INDEX